Especially for

_____

From

_____

Date

_____

Just for Girls

inspiration for a girl's heart

BARBOUR
PUBLISHING

© 2011 by Barbour Publishing, Inc.

ISBN 978-1-61626-162-7

Devotional readings are from *365 Daily Whispers of Wisdom for Girls*, published by Barbour Publishing, Inc.

Prayers by Debora Coty are from *Prayers for Daughters*, published by Barbour Publishing, Inc.

Quotes without attributes are taken from *Life's Little Book of Wisdom: Inspiration For Girls* and *Life's Little Book of Wisdom for Girls*, published by Barbour Publishing, Inc.

Scripture quotations marked KJV are taken from the King James Version of the Bible.

Scripture quotations marked CEV are taken from the New Century Version of the Bible, copyright © 2005 by Thomas Nelson, Inc. Used by permission.

Scripture quotations marked NIV are taken from the HOLY BIBLE, NEW INTERNATIONAL VERSION®. NIV®. Copyright © 1973, 1978, 1984 by International Bible Society. Used by permission of Zondervan. All rights reserved.

Scripture quotations marked NKJV are taken from the New King James Version®. Copyright © 1982 by Thomas Nelson, Inc. Used by permission. All rights reserved.

Scripture quotations marked NLT are taken from the *Holy Bible*, New Living Translation, copyright © 1996, 2004. Used by permission of Tyndale House Publishers, Inc. Wheaton, Illinois 60189, U.S.A. All rights reserved.

Scripture quotations marked NLV are taken from the Holy Bible, New Life Version, Copyright 1969, 1976, 1978, 1983, 1986, Christian Literature International, P.O. Box 777, Canby, OR 97013. Used by permission.

Scripture quotations marked MSG are from *THE MESSAGE*. Copyright © by Eugene H. Peterson 1993, 1994, 1995, 1996, 2000, 2001, 2002. Used by permission of NavPress Publishing Group.

Scripture quotations marked NASB are taken from the New American Standard Bible, © 1960, 1962, 1963, 1968, 1971, 1972, 1973, 1975, 1977, 1995 by The Lockman Foundation. Used by permission.

Published by Barbour Publishing, Inc., P.O. Box 719, Uhrichsville, Ohio 44683, www.barbourbooks.com

Our mission is to publish and distribute inspirational products offering exceptional value and biblical encouragement to the masses.

Member of the
Evangelical Christian
Publishers Association

Printed in China.

Contents

Just for Girls! . . .

No matter what the days may bring,
You can always count on one thing:
You are a princess—a daughter of the King!

Take a minute to nourish your blossoming
spirit with these inspiring and encouraging
devotions, scriptures, quotations, and prayers
that will draw you closer to God's heart and
fill your princess cup with everlasting joy!

You Are a Princess:

Assurance

*"I will be a Father to you,
and you shall be My. . .daughters,
says the LORD Almighty."*

2 CORINTHIANS 6:18 NKJV

Me, a Princess?

Don't you know?
As a child of God, you are a princess in His kingdom.
Yes, that's right—a princess!

On days when you're feeling down and need a boost of assurance, remember not only who you are—but whose you are. You belong to the King! He created you and made you into the unique, beautiful, and talented individual you are.

So what if you have one too many freckles? So what if you have short, unruly curls instead of long, silky locks? So what if you're not the best singer in the choir? God loves you just as you are—just as He made you. Your freckles. . .your hair. . .that off-key singing voice. . . these are the things that make you different from anyone else on the planet—and all were chosen just for you by the Master Creator.

The next time you look in the mirror. . .the next time you miss that high note. . .smile, and thank God for the fine job He did making you, His princess.

—Kelly Williams

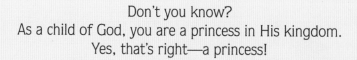

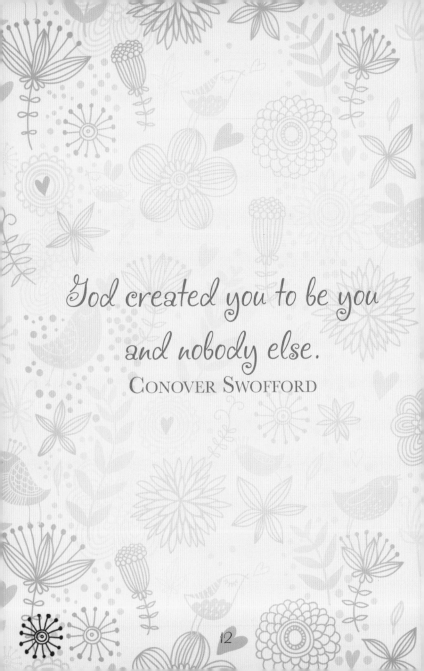

God created you to be you
and nobody else.
CONOVER SWOFFORD

An Original Design

I'm so glad You think I'm beautiful, Father.
I'm an original by the top Designer of all time!
You use only quality materials,
and Your fashions are always in style!

—Debora Coty

For we are God's masterpiece.
He has created us anew in Christ Jesus,
so we can do the good things
he planned for us long ago.

<small>EPHESIANS 2:10 NLT</small>

You Are a Masterpiece

As the Master Artist,
God signed His name on the canvas of your life.
You make Him proud.

The moment God created you, He smiled. Only the Master Artist could create a person whose eyes can see more than ten million different colors, and whose body parts function so perfectly together. He knows every hair on your head—even though you shed dozens of them every day—and every millimeter your toenails grow. He knows each of the forty million times your heart will beat this year and can identify each one of the more than two trillion red blood cells pumping through your circulatory system right now.

As proud as God was when He thought you into existence, He's even more pleased when you ask Him to make you new again by accepting Jesus Christ. That's when you—the masterpiece of His creation—become a sinless and perfected version of yourself through the grace offered by Jesus' death and resurrection.

Think of it—you're a priceless masterpiece times two! God has a wonderful future planned for His children—both here on earth and in eternity in heaven.

—Annie Tipton

When you're smiling
on the inside,
it shows on the outside.

BONNIE JENSEN

The Right Focus

Cleansers, foundation, mascara, lip gloss. . .
kindness, patience, gentleness, self-control. . .
Lord, help me to focus as much on my inner beauty
as my outer beauty.

—Debora Coty

Don't be concerned about the outward beauty of fancy hairstyles, expensive jewelry, or beautiful clothes. You should clothe yourselves instead with the beauty that comes from within, the unfading beauty of a gentle and quiet spirit, which is so precious to God.

1 PETER 3:3–4 NLT

Princess Practice:

Behavior

*No, O people, the LORD has
told you what is good,
and this is what he requires of you:
to do what is right, to love mercy,
and to walk humbly with your God.*

MICAH 6:8 NLT

Pleasing God Is Easy

We just need to follow His will and do what He asks.
It's really not hard.

Did you ever want to please your parents or grandparents, so you did something you knew they wanted you to do—like walk the dog, clean your room, or be nice to your sister? Well, God wants you to please Him, too. But what can you do to please Him?

You will always please God by doing what's right. And God gave you the Bible so you'd know what "right" is. He also gave you parents and grandparents to help guide you.

You can also please God by loving mercy. He has shown us mercy by sending His Son to die for us. In turn, you can show mercy to others by being kind and forgiving them when they do you wrong.

Last but not least, please God by being humble—by not thinking you are better, or smarter, or prettier than others. It's that easy!

Remember all that God has done for you by pleasing Him. There's nothing to it.

—Janet Lee Barton

Give the world the best you know,

and the best will come back to you.

HENRY WADSWORTH LONGFELLOW

Just Do It!

One of the promises You made in the Bible is that if children obey their parents, "it will go well with you" (see Ephesians 6:1–3 NIV). You also said it pleases You when we're obedient (see Colossians 3:20). Help me remember, Lord, when I feel like I have better things to do than listen to Mom or Dad, that obedience doesn't require feeling like it. Just doing it.

—Debora Coty

*"Now if you will obey me
and keep my covenant,
you will be my own special treasure."*

EXODUS 19:5 NLT

Going Against the Flow

**Everyone is doing it.
So why shouldn't you?**

Everybody lies. Everybody cheats. Everybody disobeys their parents. . .or do they? And even if that's true, is it okay for you to do those things?

Many people like to say that "everybody does it" to excuse their own bad behavior. But the truth is that when you are a child of God, you are expected to do His will. That means telling the truth even if no one else does. It means refusing to cheat and always obeying your parents. It means not stooping to the level of "everybody."

God's children are different because they act differently than the rest of the world. They go against the flow. They stand up for what's right. They are honest and obedient, even if being so makes them unpopular.

God treasures His children. He blesses them for their obedience. He takes care of their needs and makes sure they are happy. And best of all, He promises a wonderful reward in heaven someday.

Don't be like "everybody." Be bold. Be different. Be a child of God.

—Gale Hyatt

God has amazing plans
for your life!
Follow His lead, and you
will have no regrets!

Make Me a Mirror

Lord, make me a mirror today.
When others look at me,
I want them to see Jesus reflected in my life.

—Debora Coty

*To all who believed him and accepted him,
he gave the right to become children of God.*

JOHN 1:12 NLT

A Princess Faith:

Believing

You go before me and follow me.
You place your hand of blessing on my head.

PSALM 139:5 NLT

Never Alone

Feeling lonely?
God is with you every moment of every day!

Whenever you are feeling all alone, check out Psalm 139. The Bible says that God examines our hearts and knows everything about us. He knows when we sit down and stand up, and He even knows everything we're going to say before we ever say it. Amazing! Does that make you feel closer to God and a little less lonely? If you're not quite there yet. . .keep reading. Psalm 139 continues and tells us that no matter where we go—as high up as the heavens. . .as far as the distant side of the sea. . .in the darkness or in the light—God is always with us, no matter what!

We can never hide from Him, because He knows everything about us all of the time. He even knows how many hairs are on our heads (Luke 12:7)! So when you are feeling alone, remember that God is more than just the Creator of all things; He is your heavenly Father who knows you and wants to have a very personal relationship with you every day!

—MariLee Parrish

God's hand is always there;
once you grab it,
He'll never let go.

A Warm Heart

Jesus, when I am lonely,
thank You for being there.
It warms my heart
when You're always
happy to see me.

—Debora Coty

*But even there, if you seek GOD, your God,
you'll be able to find him if you're serious,
looking for him with your whole
heart and soul.*

DEUTERONOMY 4:29 MSG

Seek, and You Will Find

If you want God, He is there.
He is not hiding.
He truly wants to be with you.

God loves you. He truly wants a special relationship with you, but He will never force Himself upon you. He wants you to desire His presence in your life. He has promised that if you seek Him with your whole heart, you will find Him. He won't hide in hard places; you just need to go to the right place to discover Him.

Spend some time with God today. Talk to Him in prayer. Talk to Him as you would talk to your best friend—that is what He wants to be. Share your joys with Him. Share your troubles. Let Him experience everything with you. Then choose a passage from the Bible, and let God talk to you.

Seek Him with your heart—you will find Him.

—Rachel Quillin

Just believe. . .and when
you're worried, pray!
When you're lonely, pray!
When you're afraid, pray!
When you're joyful, pray!
God is waiting to hear
from you, 24/7.

Tuck It Away

My Strength and my Song, help me learn Your precious Word. I want to memorize scripture so that I can tuck it away in my heart. That way, even if there's no Bible around, You can speak to me every time and in any place I need to hear from You.

—Debora Coty

"Call to Me and I will answer you."

The Princess Cup:

Blessings

"I have loved you with an everlasting love."

A Bottomless Love

When you invite your friends to a princess tea party,
you surely don't want to run out of tea.
How about a bottomless teapot?

As you hurry to get ready for school, you pour some
breakfast cereal into your bowl and realize somebody
left you with a few drops of milk. Then you get to class,
forgetting you used up your notebook paper. Nearly
everything eventually runs out. So does anything simply
keep on giving? You'll love the answer, princess. God's
love never runs dry!

God's love is plentiful in the morning, there for you
at bedtime, and available every minute in between. Don't
worry about the next day, either, because it'll never get
down to the last few drops. There's plenty to go around.
God loves you with a bottomless love that keeps on
giving.

As you get into the day and things run out, pause and
thank God for His awesome supply of love. Enjoy! You'll
never use it up.

—Cheryl Cecil

God loves each one
of us as if there were
only one of us.

SAINT AUGUSTINE

Our Provider

Teach us about Your incredible nature through Your Hebrew names, Lord. You are Jehovah-Jireh (our Provider). You know of our needs even before we ask. Thank You for Your gracious provision.

—Debora Coty

Celebrate God all day,

every day.

PHILIPPIANS 4:4 MSG

Pure Joy!

Think about all the lovely things God has given
for your enjoyment—not just "stuff,"
but the things in life that really matter.
He has blessed you with so much
that you could have an "I've been blessed"
celebration every day of the week!

Think about some things you'd like to have. . . .
Pretty easy, right? Maybe you've been wanting a new
pair of jeans or shoes. Or maybe you'd like to have a
brand-new iPod. We always have a ready list of "stuff"
that would make us just a little happier, don't we?

But have you ever made a list—an A to Z,
everything-that's-good-in-your-life list? From the simple
to the big stuff—sunshine, your favorite food, your
lovable (and only occasionally annoying) sister or brother,
your friends, your bike, your house, your favorite family
vacation spot—you have too many blessings to name!

While we often tend to think about all of the things
we don't have, the fact is that every moment of the day,
no matter where you look, you can find at least one item
to thank God for—one blessing in your life. Now that's
reason to celebrate. . .all day long!

—Kelly Williams

There is something in every
season, in every day,
to celebrate with thanksgiving.
GLORIA GAITHER

Your Heart's Treasure

You said that where my treasure is, there will my heart be also (Matthew 6:21). But what's in my treasure chest, Lord? It's what I think about most, isn't it? That's the treasure that captures my heart. Help me make my treasure the golden kind that will last forever, not the weak and temporary kind that will crumple like aluminum foil.

—Debora Coty

I will bless the LORD at all times;
His praise shall continually be in my mouth.

PSALM 34:1 NKJV

Princess Prayer:

Heavenly Connection

*We are confident that he hears us
whenever we ask for anything that pleases him.
And since we know he hears us when we make
our requests, we also know that he will
give us what we ask for.*

1 JOHN 5:14–15 NLT

He Hears Me

God eagerly desires to answer your requests.
Don't wait any longer to talk with Him in prayer.

Did you know that God enjoys hearing us ask Him for things that please Him? When we make requests that are within His will, He hears us and will give us what we ask for.

God isn't a heavenly Santa Claus, though. Our requests for new clothes, jewelry, and cell phones aren't the prayers He's ready to answer. Instead, the prayers He's eagerly waiting to hear are the ones that you pray on behalf of someone hurting or in need. Selfless prayers are melodies He longs to hear.

Or maybe you're looking for guidance about a decision you need to make—ask God. Ask Him for the wisdom you need to live out His will every day. Ask Him to supply the things you need, having faith that He's already working everything out before you even know you have a need.

More than anything else, God wants to hear from you. Talk to Him today, and then take time to listen for His voice.

—Annie Tipton

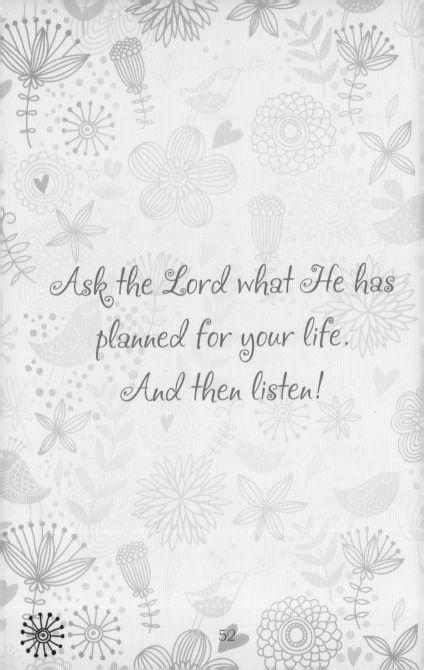

Ask the Lord what He has
planned for your life.
And then listen!

Not Just a Wish List

Giver of all good things, I don't mean to treat You as my personal Santa Claus in the sky. Help me spend just as much time thanking You and praising You as I do asking for things on my wish list.

—Debora Coty

Is any one of you in trouble?
He should pray.
Is anyone happy?
Let him sing songs of praise.

<small>JAMES 5:13 NIV</small>

Prayer and Praise

Pray to the Lord and praise Him each day.

When you want to get close to a friend, you spend lots of time with her, right? The same is true about God. To get close to Him, you spend time with Him. The best way to do that is through prayer and praise.

When you pray, you can tell God all your problems. If you are having a hard time or are in trouble—in school, with your family or friends—talk it out with God and ask for His help. Before and after reading your Bible, ask God to make His words clear to you. He listens each time you call to Him, and He will help you. God always answers prayers.

God also loves to share your happiness. When good things happen to you—like getting a good grade on a test, a raise in your allowance, or that puppy in the pet store window—remember to sing songs of praise to God. Praise and thank Him for allowing goodness in your life. Praise Him for giving you a family to love, friends to care about, and happiness. If you're having a bad day and are not sure what to praise Him for, check out the psalms and read one aloud to Him. He loves to hear His Word from his daughter's lips! Afterward, you'll feel better and so will He.

The way to grow closer to God is to share your life with Him—each day.

—Janet Lee Barton

The way to a great day:
Begin and end it
with a prayer!

A Partner in Prayer

Lord, send me a prayer partner. I want a close girlfriend to pray with as well as for. How awesome to know someone is praying especially for me!

—Debora Coty

Praise the LORD in song,
for He has done excellent things;
let this be known throughout the earth.

ISAIAH 12:5 NASB

The Princess Kingdom:

Family and Friends

*Honor thy father and thy mother, as the L*ORD
thy God hath commanded thee;
that thy days may be prolonged,
and that it may go well with thee,
*in the land which the L*ORD *thy*
God giveth thee.

DEUTERONOMY 5:16 KJV

Honor Your Parents

Respect for your parents is required by God.
He put you together for a purpose.
Obey Him, and He will bless you.

Maybe your parents are totally great. Yours is the house where all the kids want to spend their time. On the other hand, maybe you feel like your parents are trying to rule your life. Or it could be that your mom and dad fall somewhere in the middle.

The truth is that no parent is completely perfect. Parents are human, just like you. For the most part, they are trying to help you become a mature young woman. Even though you might not like everything they say or do, you must remember that God has a reason for putting you together. He expects you to honor your parents—to respect and obey them.

When all things go well, thank God. If you are struggling, turn your situation over to God. You might be surprised to discover that it's you who needs to change.

Above all, honor your parents, and enjoy God's blessing that follows.

—Rachel Quillin

Thank your parents for
all they do for you.
And always remember
them in your prayers.

Understanding Unconditional Love

Help me appreciate my family, Gracious Father, for they are Your way of helping me begin to understand Your unconditional love. Amen.

—Debora Coty

Two are better than one;
because they have a good reward
for their labour.

ECCLESIASTES 4:9 KJV

Stick Together

Your friends are priceless.
You are important to them, and they to you.
Guard this treasure.

Can you imagine how sad and frightened Naomi must have felt as she prepared to leave Moab and return to Bethlehem? She dared not hope Ruth or Orpah would accompany her, and she had no one else. The life ahead would be lonely and hard.

Ruth saw that Naomi needed her. In her heart she realized that Naomi also had much to offer. It's true there were many differences between them. They probably disagreed at times, and maybe they even got on each other's nerves, but they stuck together, and both women were rewarded.

Are you ever tempted to turn your back on your friend? Maybe you're embarrassed by an outfit she's wearing, or maybe she laughed at your shoes. Has a new friend joined your tight twosome and you're feeling crowded? Perhaps your friend has developed a new interest that really doesn't excite you. Remember: There will always be differences between you. That's what makes you special. But you're a lot more alike than you realize. Don't abandon your friend. She's a gift from God, and you need each other.

—Rachel Quillin

To have a good friend is one
of the highest delights of
life; to be a good friend is one
of the noblest undertakings.

UNKNOWN

Much-Needed Flavor

*You said Your children are the salt and light of the
world (Matthew 5:13–14), much needed to add
flavor to blandness and lead the way through the dark.
Help me, Lord, to pass the salt and hold my candle
high for those in my neighborhood and social circles.*

—Debora Coty

There is a friend who sticks closer than a brother.

PROVERBS 18:24 AMP

The Princess Manual:

God's Word

*Your word is a lamp to my feet
and a light for my path.*

PSALM 119:105 NIV

70

Let It Shine!

God's Word is like a light in a dark world.
Knowing it will give you the tools
you need to see clearly in the dark times.

When the lights are off, it's easy to stumble. You can falter in your step, stub your toe, or step on something painful in your efforts to find your way. The same is true when you are in the dark spiritually. God's Word is a lamp that will shine the light onto your path as you walk through life. Its guidance will help you avoid a painful walk through the dark.

Make it a priority to memorize God's Word. Being able to call to mind scriptural truth and to know the words of God helps dark things become very clear. The verses you learn will help you when temptation comes your way. They will comfort you through troubled times. They will remind you of how you can please God in your daily life. They are like a light in a dark place. Let God's Word light the way for you in the darkness of the world. Let it shine!

—Nicole O'Dell

People are like stained-glass windows:
They sparkle and shine when the sun is out,
but when the darkness sets in,
their true beauty is revealed only if
there is light within.

ELIZABETH KÜBLER-ROSS

Supernatural Best Friend

Just like I wouldn't dream of going twenty-four hours without hearing from my best friend, help me commit to reading Your Word every single day. After all, the Bible is like text messages from my supernatural best friend.

—Debora Coty

*Great peace have those who love Your law,
and nothing causes them to stumble.*

PSALM 119:165 NKJV

Love God's Word

The peace that passes all understanding can be yours.
Love God's Word and learn it.

Do you ever feel uncomfortable because some of your
friends want you to do something you don't think you
should? Or have you felt confused because you aren't
sure what it is you should be doing? Do you feel worried
that you might do something wrong just to please
others? Do you need direction from a master navigator?

To figure out which way to go on the road of life,
check out God's Word. It has all the direction you need.
The more you read and study your Bible, the better you
will know what you should and shouldn't do. And His
Word will also give you the strength to tell yourself or
your friends no when you need to.

Want peace of mind? Just pick up your Bible and
then talk to Jesus—the Prince of peace. They'll give you
good directions to follow, the strength to obey, and the
peace that comes from choosing the right path.

—Janet Lee Barton

Unsure of something?
God's Word will tell you
exactly what to do!

Love Letters

Lord, how awesome it is to know that You think about me every minute of every day. Help me to faithfully set aside ten minutes a day to read Your love letters (the Bible) and think about You. You made me and gave me everything I have. It's the least I can do.

—Debora Coty

But if anyone obeys his word,
God's love is truly made complete in him.
This is how we know we are in him.

1 JOHN 2:5 NIV

Princess Gifts:

Talents

*For this reason, I ask you to keep using
the gift God gave you.
It came to you when I laid my hands on you
and prayed that God would use you.*

2 Timothy 1:6 NLV

Stir Up Your Gifts!

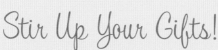

God gave you very special gifts, talents, and abilities. You can use those gifts to bring others into His kingdom.

Isn't it fun to think about the special talents God has given you? Maybe you can sing or play an instrument. Perhaps you enjoy acting or dancing—and love to perform on the "big stage." Maybe you prefer to scribble down your thoughts in your journal or write funny little poems to make people smile.

Remember, all of these abilities come from God, and He wants you to stir them up! Keep practicing. . .keep working at them! And while you're doing this, don't compare yourself to others. So what if someone else is a little better at something than you are? The Lord gave your friends gifts, too; and He wants those special abilities to be used. All of His children are uniquely created, and it's a blast to watch those talents grow!

The King of kings took the time to give you—His princess—gifts. Unwrap each one and use it to His glory!

—Janice Hanna

Use what talents you possess:
The woods would be very
silent if no birds sang there
except those that sang best.

HENRY VAN DYKE

Can Do!

There are so many people who have so little, Lord, and You have given me so much. Help me to reach out to help others. Even if I don't have extra money to give, I have arms and legs that can do.

—Debora Coty

Each of you has been blessed with one of God's many wonderful gifts to be used in the service of others. So use your gift well.

1 PETER 4:10 CEV

Busy Bees

Everyone has a job to do.
God has given you talents and special interests
that will enable you to do what He wants you to do.

Everyone is different. We all have different interests and abilities. Some girls are musically talented; some are creative in other ways. Some do a great job with little children, and still others are better suited for different activities. No job is better or more important than another. God has designed it so that all of the jobs work together perfectly.

In a beehive, each bee needs to do his own job so that the honey can be made. The bees can't all be drones (husbands to the queen bee). They all can't be worker bees, either. And they all can't be queens. Each kind of bee is needed in order to produce the sweet, rich honey from the comb.

The body of Christ is like a honeycomb. What is it that God has set aside to be your special role? God asks you to do your best in whatever work you are given. Do it as though you are doing it for Him.

—Nicole O'Dell

Be the best you
that you can be!

Like Christmas Gifts

Dear God, thank You for the special gifts You've given just to me—my heart, my mind, my unique talents and abilities. Like Christmas gifts, I want to open and enjoy them, not stuff them in my closet or under my bed to be ignored and forgotten.

—Debora Coty

*Just think—you don't need a thing,
you've got it all!
All God's gifts are right in front of you.*

1 CORINTHIANS 1:7 MSG

Princess Praise:

Thankfulness

*I call to the L*ORD*, who is worthy of praise,*
and I am saved from my enemies.

PSALM **18:3** NIV

W for Worthy!

Can you hear it? The rocks along the edge of the road. . .
they're singing the praises of God!

Did you know that we were created to worship God?
It's true! If we don't praise Him, the rocks will begin to
shout out praises to the King of kings. (Can you imagine
the rocks bursting out in joyful song? Wouldn't that be
something to hear!) We're going to be praising the Lord
for all eternity, so we'd better get started now.

God is worthy to be praised! He's amazing and
awesome. He created the whole world—just by speaking
it into existence. He sent His Son to die on the cross—
proving His love for us, once and for all. Yes, God truly
loves us, and that alone makes Him worthy!

A daughter of the King can't say enough good things
about her Father. Why, she brags on Him all day long!
She sings His praises to everyone who will listen. So let
a song of praise fill your heart today, princess. If you
don't, the rocks will surely begin to shout!

—Janice Hanna

Send up a big "thank You"
to God for making the earth
and everything in it.

Shout from the Rooftops

Thank You for being You. The Great I Am.
The same yesterday, today, and tomorrow.
I want to shout from the rooftops:
My God is an AWESOME God!

—Debora Coty

Always give thanks for all things to God the Father in the name of our Lord Jesus Christ.

EPHESIANS 5:20 NLV

A Thankful Heart

When things don't quite go your way, instead of feeling sorry for yourself, think of everything in your life that's good—there are a lot of wonderful things in this life of yours! Then say a great big thanks to God.

Bad days? We all have them. And you've been there with. . .the haircut that didn't turn out like the picture, the reprimand from your teacher for talking in class, the less-than-perfect grade on your spelling test, and the bruised knees from your embarrassing trip over your chair in Sunday school.

We can't always control things that go wrong, but we can control our reaction to those things. So the next time you have a bad day, think about the wonderful things in your life—like your wonderful family, your cuddly pet, your best friend, your bedroom that's decorated just the way you like it—and you'll find yourself bouncing back fast from your sour mood.

And last but not least, thank God for all the good stuff in your life. He'll be happy to hear from you!

—Kelly Williams

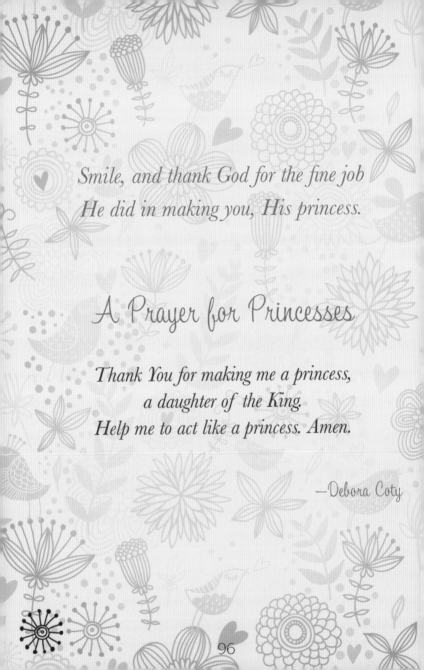

Smile, and thank God for the fine job
He did in making you, His princess.

A Prayer for Princesses

Thank You for making me a princess,
a daughter of the King.
Help me to act like a princess. Amen.

—Debora Coty